Y0-BXV-900

The ABC's of Exercise

By Andrea Lott &
Tricia Murphy Madden

Illustrated by Jerry Steffen, Jr.

Seattle, Washington
Portland, Oregon
Denver, Colorado
Vancouver, B.C.
Scottsdale, Arizona
Minneapolis, Minnesota

ISBN: 978-1-59849-176-0

Printed in the United States of America
Library of Congress Control Number: 2014922681

Illustrations by Jerry Steffen, Jr.
Design by Soundview Design Studio

Requests for such permissions should be addressed to:

Peanut Butter Publishing
943 NE Boat Street
Seattle, Washington 98105
206-860-4900
www.peanutbutterpublishing.com

To our children and
the millions of children
whose heart, brains and
bodies are our future.

Are you ready
to exercise?

Bring lots of energy
because you're going to
work from your head
all the way to
your toes.

Come along as
we do the ABC's
of exercise.

Arm starts with A so reach yours way up high.

Bend down low

and
touch
your toes.

Clap your hands

and shake your hips.

Now let's see your best **Down Dog.**

Extend
one leg
up to
the sky.
Now try
the other
side.

Walk your hands to your Feet,
then stand up big and tall.
Flexibility is Fun!

Gallop like a horse and

Giddeeup

Next, Hop Hop Hop like
a bunny -
back
and
forth
and
side
to
side.

Watch me,
I can twirl
like an
Ice skater.

Jump
up
and
down
then do
some
Jumping
Jacks.

Kick
your legs
5
and lift
your
Knees.

Your Lungs are working,

aren't you pleased?

Moving
is important,
WOW
it builds
big
Muscles.

Plus eating **N**utritious foods is good for your brain –

which acts like a muscle.

Oranges, Oats and Okra are all healthy Options.

Can you think of other nutritious foods?

Push-ups are fun too.
Lower down and
Push back up,
they're not
so easy to do.

Now stay in Plank, don't
move a muscle. Jump to your
feet and do the hustle!

Quick, Quick run in place.

Go so fast you'll
win the race.

Take a breath and Rest.

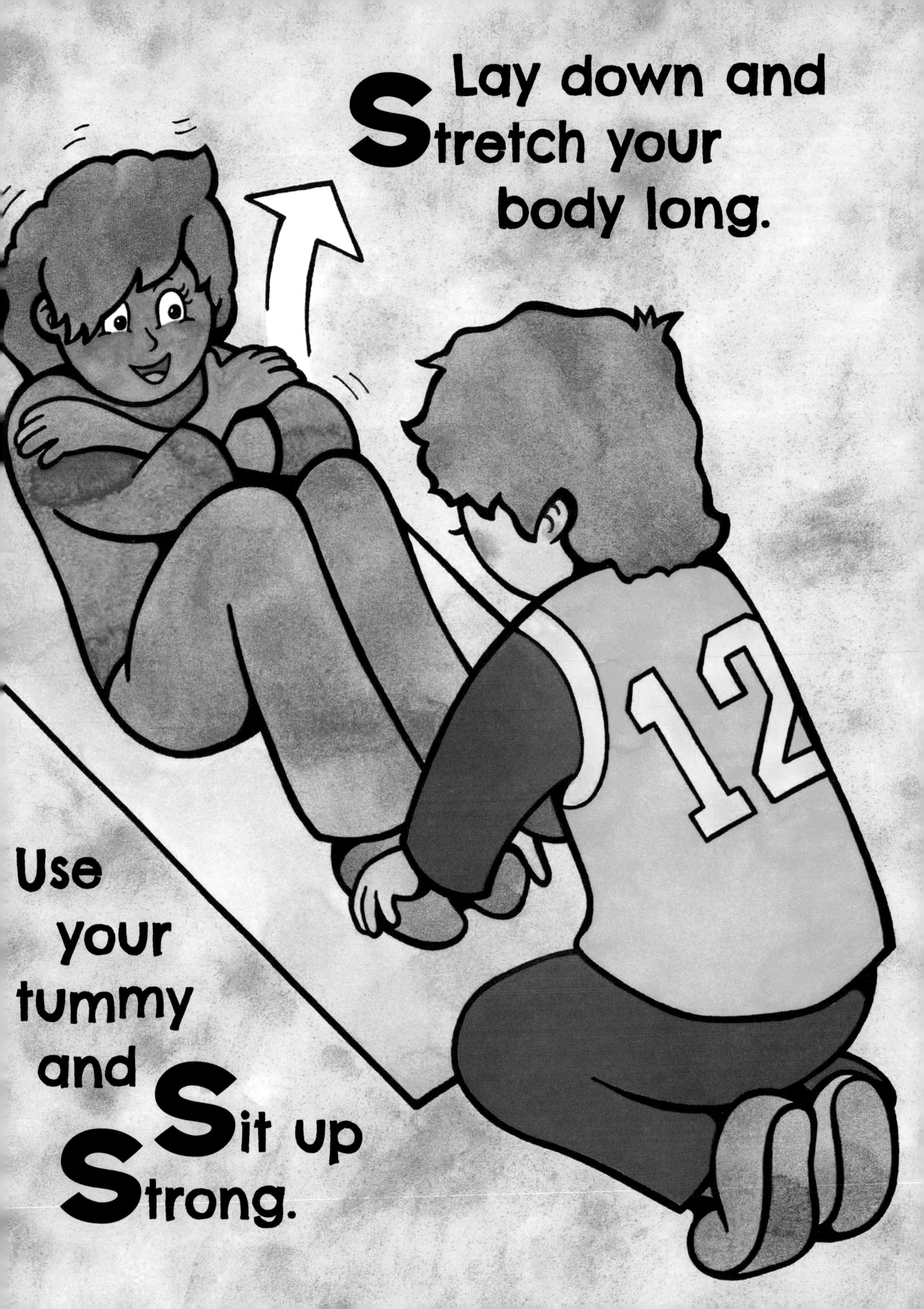
Lay down and
Stretch your
body long.
12
Use
your
tummy
and Sit up
Strong.

Tug on an imaginary rope -
pretend you're climbing a Tree.

UP
UP
UP you go!

You've earned a gold star –
Victory!

Walk or
Wiggle,
which
one
makes
you
giggle?

XERCISE
E
eXercise
can be fun,
you better ask
someone how
to spell that
one!

But now I can't stop Yawning.

Exercise is good for me,
but don't forget to get your
ZZZ's.
A
ZZZZZ
Tomorrow
we can try
Z
again
and these
words will be a breeze.

As avid exercisers, mothers and native Seattlites, Andrea Lott and Tricia Murphy Madden are friends, entrepreneurs and workout buddies on a mission to spread the word about exercise and healthy living in a fun and educational way. *The ABC's of Exercise* gives parents, teachers and caregivers of toddlers and young children a hands-on solution for structured play and exercise.

Tricia Murphy Madden is both a mother and fitness instructor. For the last two decades she has taught group fitness classes and workshops from west coast gyms to fitness conferences around the world. The star of 15 exercise DVD's, an American Council on Exercise Faculty Member, and a former gym owner, Tricia is a contributor to numerous publications including Redbook, AOL Health and the Fitness Journal. Tricia brings her knowledge and passion to the pages of *The ABC's of Exercise* to help children experience fitness at an early age, and enjoy it for life. She currently resides in Seattle with her husband, Shawn, 4-year old daughter, Tabitha, and dog, Lica.

Andrea Lott, unleashed her love of exercise at the age of eighteen months, at the Little Gym, and went on to become a Division I collegiate gymnast. As a mother, cookbook author and former management consultant, she continues to be passionate about exercise, being fit and healthy living. She hopes *The ABC's of Exercise* fun will help young children develop habits that will last a lifetime. Andrea is a Yale University graduate and lives on Mercer Island with her husband, Jordan, and 2-year old daughter, Audrey, who also loves the Little Gym!

Jerry Steffen, Jr. is a Seattle-area free-lance artist. Born with complete hearing loss, Jerry uses his art as therapy. With a twist of fate, Jerry got in to watercolor painting and was a vendor at the Pike Place Market from 2000-2012. While he typically draws landscape, animal, fantasy and floral art, *The ABC's of Exercise* is Jerry's first children's book.

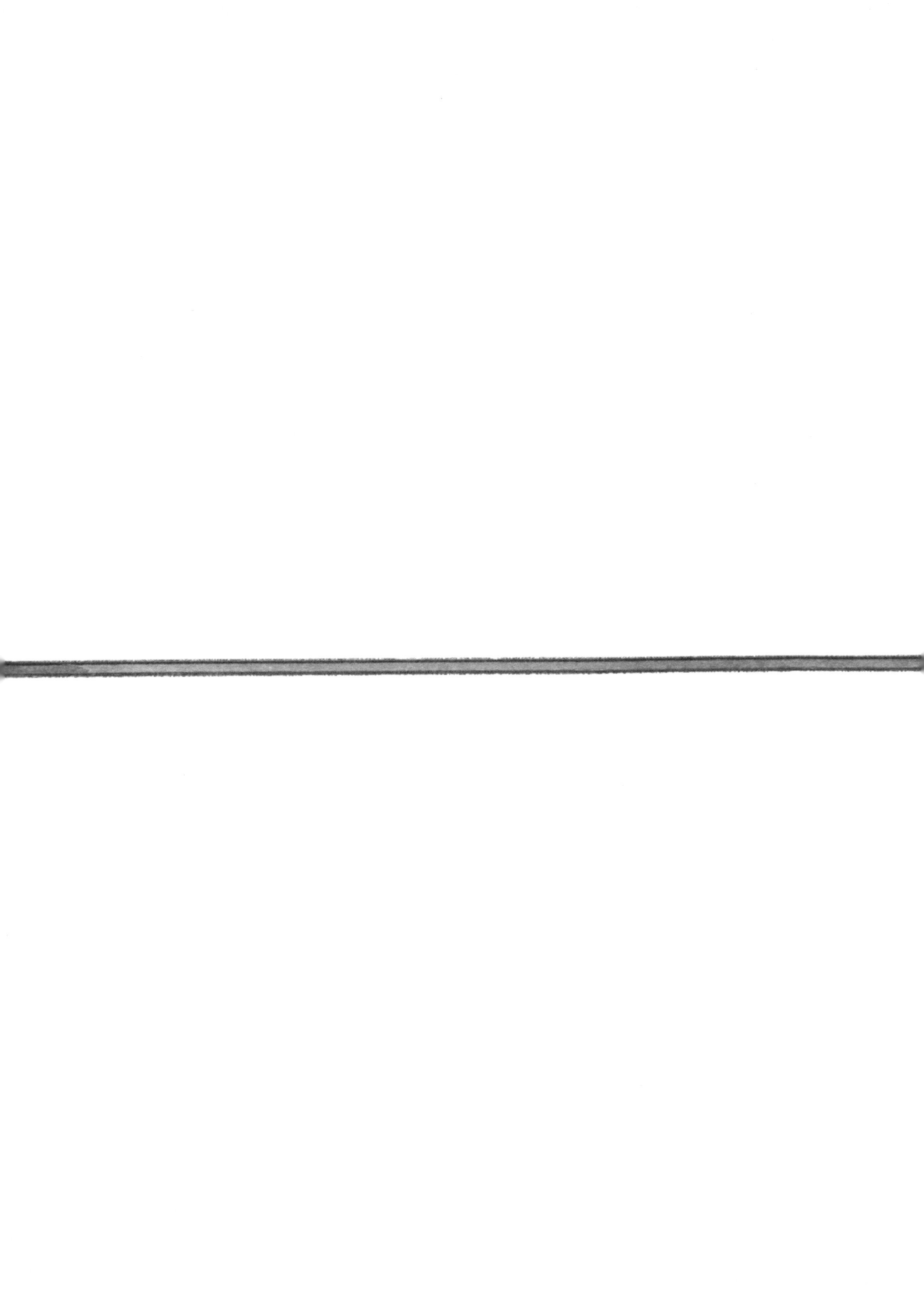